About Skill Builders
Reading
Comprehension Grade 5

Welcome to Skill Builders *Reading Comprehension* for fifth grade. This book is designed to improve children's reading comprehension skills through focused practice. The book's eye-catching graphics and engaging topics entice even reluctant readers. Each full-color workbook contains grade-level-appropriate passages and exercises based on national standards to help ensure that children master basic skills before progressing.

More than 70 pages of activities cover essential comprehension strategies, such as inferring, sequencing, and finding the main idea and supporting details. The workbook also contains questions and activities to help children build their vocabularies.

The Skill Builders series offers workbooks that are perfect for keeping children current during the school year or preparing them for the next grade.

Credits:
Content Editor: Elizabeth Swenson
Copy Editor: Beki Benning
Layout, Cover Design, and Inside Illustrations: Nick Greenwood

www.carsondellosa.com
Carson-Dellosa Publishing LLC
Greensboro, North Carolina

Printed in the USA • All rights reserved.

ISBN 978-1-93602-333-2
02-086121151

Table of Contents

Suggested Reading List

Anderson, Laurie Halse
Fever 1793

Avi
The True Confessions of Charlotte Doyle

Balliett, Blue
Chasing Vermeer

Barry, Dave and Ridley Pearson
Peter and the Starcatchers

Baum, L. Frank (adapted by Michael Cavallaro)
L. Frank Baum's The Wizard of Oz: The Graphic Novel

Berger, Melvin and Gilda Berger
The Real Vikings: Craftsmen, Traders, and Fearsome Raiders

Cassedy, Sylvia
Behind the Attic Wall

Cherry, Lynne and Gary Braasch
How We Know What We Know About Our Changing Climate: Scientists and Kids Explore Global Warming

Conrad, Pam
My Daniel

Cooper, Susan
The Dark Is Rising series

Creech, Sharon
Chasing Redbird

Dahl, Roald
The BFG; Charlie and the Chocolate Factory

DiCamillo, Kate
Because of Winn-Dixie

DuPrau, Jeanne
The City of Ember

Erdrich, Louise
The Birchbark House

Farley, Walter
The Black Stallion

Frank, Anne
Anne Frank: The Diary of a Young Girl

George, Jean Craighead
My Side of the Mountain; Julie of the Wolves

Gray, Elizabeth Janet
Adam of the Road

Hautzig, Esther
The Endless Steppe: Growing Up in Siberia

Konigsburg, E. L.
From the Mixed-up Files of Mrs. Basil E. Frankweiler

Lewis, C. S.
The Chronicles of Narnia series

Lord, Bette Bao
In the Year of the Boar and Jackie Robinson

McKinley, Robin
The Hero and the Crown; The Door in the Hedge

Naylor, Phyllis Reynolds
Shiloh

O'Dell, Scott
Island of the Blue Dolphins

Raskin, Ellen
The Westing Game

Sachar, Louis
Holes

Speare, Elizabeth George
Calico Captive

Stanley, Diane
Michelangelo

Stead, Rebecca
When You Reach Me

Winthrop, Elizabeth
The Castle in the Attic

Yep, Laurence
The Tiger's Apprentice

The Olmecs

Read the passage. Then, answer the questions.

The Olmecs were native people of modern-day Mexico and Central America. The Olmecs were one of the earliest cultures. They mostly lived in a coastal area along the Gulf of Mexico.

The Olmec people made huge sculpted stone heads. Many of these stone heads still exist today. Some are as large as 8 feet (2.4 m) tall and weigh as much as 40 tons (36 mt)! These huge pieces were carved and moved over many miles. No one knows for sure how the Olmecs moved such large and heavy stones or why they moved them so far. The stone heads mix features of humans and animals such as jaguars. Some scientists think that the stones were meant to be symbols of Olmec rulers.

The Olmecs are also well known for their skills in architecture, pottery, art, mathematics, and astronomy. Their understanding of astronomy may have helped them design a calendar very similar to the one used today.

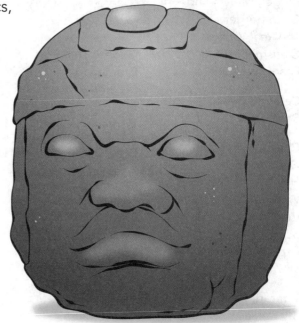

1. Where did most of the Olmecs live?

   A. a coastal area along the Gulf of Mexico
   B. a coastal area along California
   C. central Mexico
   D. South America

2. What did the stone heads look like?

   _____

   _____

   _____

3. Write *T* if a statement is true. Write *F* if a statement is false.

   _____ The Olmecs were skilled in architecture, pottery, art, mathematics, and astronomy.

   _____ The Olmecs did not use a calendar.

   _____ The Olmecs lived in modern-day South America.

   _____ We do not know how or why the Olmecs moved the stone heads.

4. What do some scientists think the stone heads symbolized?

   _____

   _____

5. What are the Olmecs also well known for?

   _____

   _____

   _____

Eldorado

Read the poem. Then, answer the questions.

Eldorado
by Edgar Allan Poe

Gaily bedight*,
A **gallant** knight,
In sunshine and in shadow,
Had journeyed long,
Singing a song,
In search of Eldorado.

But he grew old—
This knight so bold—
And o'er his heart a shadow
Fell as he found
No spot of ground
That looked like Eldorado.

And, as his strength
Failed him at length,
He met a pilgrim shadow—
"Shadow," said he,
"Where can it be—
This land of Eldorado?"

"Over the Mountains
Of the Moon,
Down the Valley of the Shadow,
Ride, boldly ride,"
The shade replied,—
"If you seek for Eldorado!"

* colorfully dressed

1. What does **gallant** mean in the poem?

    A. tired and weak
    B. foolish and unwise
    C. noble and brave
    D. cowardly and scared

2. Do you think that the knight ever finds Eldorado? Why or why not?

    _____

    _____

    _____

3. What mood does Poe create with this poem?

    _____

4. Circle three words from the poem that help create this mood.

5. El Dorado is a legendary golden city that is filled with treasure and precious jewels. Many explorers have searched for the city, but it has never been found. Knowing this, what do you think Poe's message is in "Eldorado"?

    A. You should pursue your dreams, no matter what.
    B. You should not waste your life chasing a dream that cannot be accomplished.
    C. Either A. or B.
    D. none of the above

Fact or Opinion

Read each passage. Read each statement. Write *F* if a statement is a fact. Write *O* if a statement is an opinion.

A fact is a detail that is real and can be proven. An opinion is a belief that is personal and cannot be proven.

The Great Barrier Reef

Many people consider Australia's Great Barrier Reef one of the seven natural wonders of the world. It is the largest coral structure in the world and the largest structure made by living organisms.

The Great Barrier Reef consists mostly of coral, a rocklike substance made by thousands of tiny animals. These tiny animals are called *polyps*. When the polyps are born, they reproduce, eat, and eventually die. New coral is slowly added to the reef through this process.

The reef's shape and color are always changing. These changes are caused by many factors. People, harmful animals, and changes in the environment can alter and damage the reef. It is very fragile, and it is sensitive to both pollution and fishing.

1. __F__ The tiny animals that make the Great Barrier Reef are called *polyps*.

2. __O__ People should not be allowed to visit the reef.

3. __F__ It is a good thing so many polyps are in the reef.

4. __F__ The Great Barrier Reef is the world's largest coral structure.

5. __F__ People can alter or damage the Great Barrier Reef.

Tropical Rain Forests

Tropical rain forests are found near the equator. Rain forests are well named; rain falls almost every day! Tropical rain forests usually do not get hotter than 93°F (34°C) or cooler than 68°F (20°C). Tropical rain forests have many kinds of dense vegetation, including trees, vines, shrubs, and bright, colorful flowers. About half of the world's species of plants and animals live in tropical rain forests.

The world's tropical rain forests are in great danger. They are cut down to provide timber and firewood. The cleared land is used for homes, roads, farms, and factories. Some areas are cleared for the mining of oil and valuable minerals. The habitats of thousands of species of animals and plants have already vanished. The way of life for many people who live in the rain forests is also threatened by these changes.

6. __O__ There is too much vegetation in the rain forests.

7. __F__ Tropical rain forests are wet.

8. __O__ All development in tropical rain forests should stop.

9. __F__ A tropical rain forest is a densely packed area of trees and plants.

10. __O__ Tropical rain forests are interesting to study.

Nine Lives

Read the passage. Then, answer the questions.

Do you believe cats have nine lives? If they do, then a cat named Scarlett may have used a few of her lives all at once.

Scarlett was a **stray** cat surviving in an old, vacant building in New York. One day, the building caught fire. Most animals would have tried to quickly escape. But, Scarlett had five kittens to protect. As the fire got bigger, Scarlett ignored the danger. One by one, she carried her kittens to safety. By the time Scarlett saved the last kitten, her fur was badly burned, and her eyes were swollen shut.

A kind firefighter found the kittens and looked for their mother. Even though Scarlett could not see him, she trusted his voice and let him pick her up. He put her in a box with her babies. She could not see her kittens, so she counted them by touching each one's nose.

Scarlett and her kittens were rushed to an animal hospital where it took almost three months for them to heal. Scarlett's heroic story was reported in the local newspapers. Many people wanted to adopt Scarlett and her kittens. A committee at the hospital made sure that they were all adopted into good homes.

Scarlett's calico fur grew back, and her eyes opened wide once again. In her new home, she played with tissue paper balls, paper bags, and string. She rested on the windowsill. She did not act as if she were famous. She was just happy to live in a safe home with loving owners. To prove it, she purred loudly when her owners were near. Scarlett was a true survivor.

1. Choose another good title for this story. *(handwritten: 10 6% 9/12)*

   A. Too Many Cats
   B. A Firefighter Saves a Building
   C. The Cat's Meow
   D. A Mother's Love *(circled)*

2. Which of the following best defines the word **stray**?

   A. homeless   B. wild *(A circled)*
   C. tame   D. dangerous

3. Number the following events in the order that they happened.

   5 Scarlett and her kittens were adopted.

   4 The cats were taken to an animal hospital.

   1 An empty building caught fire.

   2 Scarlett carried out each kitten.

   3 A firefighter found the kittens.

4. Why do you think Scarlett let the firefighter pick her up?
   (handwritten: The firefighter was nice to her kittens. fire)

5. In what state did this story take place? *(handwritten: New York)*

6. How many kittens did Scarlett have? *(handwritten: 5)*

7. How long did it take the cats to heal? *(handwritten: 3 moyths)*

Reading Graphs

Read the passage. Then, use the graphs to answer the questions.

Scientists often share the results of their experiments through the use of graphs. It is important for scientists to be able to make and read graphs so that they can effectively share their data with others. Although scientists use many different types of graphs, the following are common types: the bar graph and the line graph.

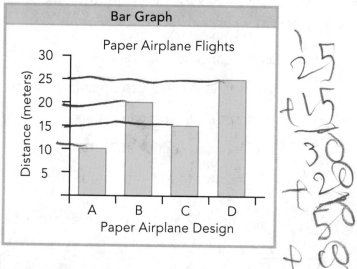

Bar Graph

Paper Airplane Flights

1. How many paper airplane designs were tested?

   60

2. Why do you think scientists like to show their data with bar graphs?

   to see how many paper airplanes.

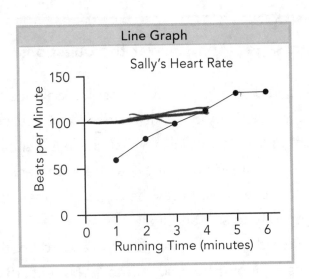

Line Graph

Sally's Heart Rate

(Graph: y-axis "Beats per Minute" from 0 to 150; x-axis "Running Time (minutes)" from 0 to 6)

3. At how many minutes did Sally's heart rate increase to 100 beats per minute?

   4

4. How long did it take for Sally's heart rate to become constant?

   5 and 6

5. According to the graph, what was Sally's peak heart rate?

   125

6. Why do you think scientists like to show their data with line graphs?

   ? |

Chambered Nautilus

Read the passage. Then, answer the questions.

The chambered nautilus is a living fossil. It belongs to a group of animals called *cephalopods.* It is related to octopuses, squids, and cuttlefish. Unlike its cousins, the nautilus has a shell on its outside. The shell is made of many chambers. The animal lives in the outermost chamber. It uses the other chambers for its *buoyancy,* or ability to sink and float.

The chambered nautilus lives in the Indian and South Pacific oceans. It lives at depths from 60 feet to 1,500 feet (18 m to 457 m) along reef walls. On dark nights, it travels closer to the surface of the water. There it eats tiny fish, shrimp, and molted, or shed, lobster shells.

The chambered nautilus cannot change color or squirt ink like its relatives, but it does have arms. Two rows of 80 to 100 small tentacles surround its head. None have suckers to hold prey, but each can touch and taste.

The chambered nautilus lives longer than other cephalopods, sometimes up to 20 years! It also reproduces more often during its lifetime than an octopus. It attaches eggs to rocks, coral, or the seafloor. Each egg takes about one year to hatch.

1. Where do chambered nautiluses live?

   Indian and South
   Pacific oceans.

2. Describe a chambered nautilus.

   Has a shell on the
   out side. It has many
   chambers.

3. What do chambered nautiluses eat?

   Tiny fish, shrimp, and
   molted or shed, lobster
   shells.

4. In the passage, circle the words that describe how nautiluses are the same as other cephalopods.

5. In the passage, underline the words that describe how nautiluses are different from other cephalopods.

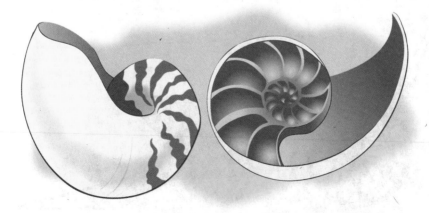

Early Pioneer Travel

Read the passage. Then, answer the questions.

American pioneers followed several different routes on their way west. Pioneers from New England traveled across New York on the Mohawk Trail. Another route went through the Cumberland Gap, a natural pass in the Appalachian Mountains. It ends near where Kentucky, Tennessee, and Virginia meet. In 1775, Daniel Boone led about 30 woodsmen to cut the Wilderness Road through parts of Virginia and Tennessee to the Cumberland Gap in Kentucky.

The first groups of settlers used these trails to cross the Appalachian Mountains in the late 1700s. Usually, a pioneer family joined several other families to move west. Some traveled on foot, carrying only a rifle, an ax, and a few supplies. But, most went by wagon. Whichever way they traveled, they did not take many belongings, especially anything that could be found along the way. For food, pioneers hunted, fished, and ate dried **staples** they carried with them.

The pioneers were only able to travel short distances every day. Most trips took several weeks.

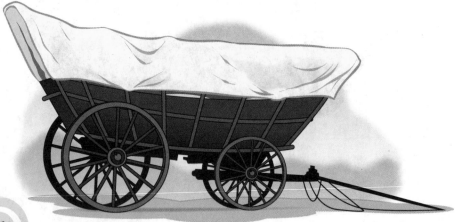

1. What does the word **staples** mean in the passage?

   A. small pieces of metal used to hold papers together
   B. small metal loops
   C. basic food supplies
   D. fresh fruit

2. Where does the Cumberland Gap end?

   Kentucky

3. How did pioneers get food?

   hunt, fish, and ate
   dried staples (basic
   food supplies)

4. How long did most trips take?

   A. several days
   B. several weeks
   C. several months
   D. several years

5. Who cut the Wilderness Road?

   woodsmen.

6. When did the first groups of settlers travel west?

   late 1700s.

Snow

Read the story. Then, answer the questions.

The landscape was a soft, swirling whiteness. Snow fell gently, blurring the world into a circle. Nina and Stella were outside with a crystal chart trying to identify snowflake types. This winter, they had already identified stellar dendrites, hexagonal plates, and needle crystals. Today, they hoped to find either the spatial dendrites or column crystals.

Stella held a **smattering** of flakes on a piece of black fabric. Nina had taken off one mitten and put it in her pocket. She held the magnifying glass with her bare hand. The girls heard a muffled noise and looked up.

The blowing snow temporarily blinded them, preventing them from seeing the large white shape leaping across the yard. *Wham!* The dog barreled into both girls. Nina fell backward into a snowbank and came up sputtering. "Down, Tiny!" she demanded. "Get off me!" Her hand was wet, red, and icy.

The magnifying glass was nowhere to be seen. Stella had fallen facedown. Tiny's hind legs were in the middle of Stella's back, preventing her from getting to her feet. Nina threw her mitten away from Stella. Tiny leaped off Stella's back to get the mitten. Fetch was Tiny's favorite game.

1. What effect did the falling snow have on the landscape?

   _____

   _____

2. What does the word **smattering** mean?

   A. something that was smashed

   B. a sound

   C. one piece of something

   D. a small collection of items

3. What prevented the girls from seeing the dog?

   _____

4. What happened when Tiny barreled into Nina?

   _____

   _____

5. Why was Nina's hand wet, red, and icy?

   A. She took off her mitten to hold the magnifying glass.

   B. She was yelling at Tiny.

   C. Stella had fallen down.

   D. She dropped her magnifying glass.

6. What prevented Stella from getting out of the snow?

   _____

   _____

   _____

That's Fantastic

Read each statement. Write _R_ if a statement is reality. Write _F_ if a statement is fantasy.

If a statement could happen, it is reality. If a statement could never happen, it is fantasy.

1. _____ My dog, Petey, loves to eat ham sandwiches. He tries to swipe mine whenever he can.

2. _____ Lana's feet were sore. Walking with the dinosaurs through the museum all afternoon was wearing holes in her shoes.

3. _____ Ping leaned back against his pillow and smiled. He loved it when Sparky, his pet turtle, read him a bedtime story.

4. _____ Every night after dinner, Madoc's responsibility was loading and unloading the dishwasher.

5. _____ Seth enjoyed spending time with his friend, Ibit. He wished he could spend time at Ibit's house, but the atmosphere on Jupiter was deadly to humans.

6. _____ Adrian was upset. He had fallen and skinned his knee for the second time in a week.

7. _____ Will enjoyed playing with his soccer team. They did not score any points in the past three games, but they always tried their best. Will liked playing with all of his friends.

8. _____ Quinn was having a hard time walking barefoot across the lava. She put her toes in a river to snuff out the flames.

9. _____ Irina made an incredible sand sculpture at the beach. She was sure it would win one of the contest prizes.

10. _____ Luke loved sitting in the hot tub. On a clear night, he could see one or two shooting stars cross the sky.

11. Write one statement that is **reality**.

_____

_____

_____

12. Write one statement that is **fantasy**.

_____

_____

_____

_____

_____

Kudzu

Read the passage. Then, answer the questions.

In 1876, some Japanese immigrants brought a plant called kudzu to Philadelphia, Pennsylvania. Kudzu had beautiful, big leaves. Its purple flowers smelled great. People liked the plant. But, nobody knew how much damage this vine could do.

Farmers in the southeastern United States planted kudzu in their fields for their cows to eat. The kudzu would grow back very quickly. Kudzu can grow 60 feet (18 m) in a year. It can even grow as much as 1 foot (30 cm) a day. It seemed better than hay.

During the 1930s and 1940s, the government paid farmers to plant kudzu in their fields. Kudzu stops soil **erosion**. It prevents land from wearing away. But, it also grows everywhere, especially in the humid southeastern states. It covers telephone poles, hills, houses, and old cars. It quickly spreads into forests and along roadsides. It kills trees and plants by covering them and blocking the sunlight they need to survive.

In 1953, the government wanted people to stop planting kudzu. The vine was getting out of control. It was damaging forests and land. People were not happy with it anymore.

It is not easy to stop kudzu. Plant poisons do not work on it. Sometimes, they even make it grow better! Also, it is hard to pull kudzu out of the ground because the roots grow so deep.

People have found other uses for kudzu, though. It can be made into baskets, paper, and feed for goats and cows. People now know that they may have to live with kudzu for many years to come.

1. What is the main idea of the second paragraph?

    A. Farmers planted kudzu in the southeastern United States.
    B. Kudzu grows quickly.
    C. Cows like to eat kudzu.
    D. Farmers liked kudzu because it grew back quickly after
        cows ate it.

2. Number the following events in the order that they
    happened.

    _____ The government wanted people to stop
          planting kudzu.

    _____ Some Japanese immigrants brought kudzu to
          Philadelphia, Pennsylvania.

    _____ Farmers thought kudzu was a great thing to plant.

    _____ Kudzu started to spread across the southeastern
          United States.

    _____ People began to find other uses for kudzu.

3. Which of the following best defines the word **erosion**?

    A. wearing away   B. digging up
    C. thickness   D. spreading

4. Why do you think kudzu grows so well in the southeastern
    United States?

    A. because kudzu came from Japan
    B. because farmers planted so much of it
    C. because the weather is sunny, warm, and humid
    D. all of the above

Cesar Chavez

Read the passage. Then, answer the questions.

Cesar Chavez was an important man to farm workers. There is even a holiday for him in California. It is on March 31, his birthday.

Chavez was born on a farm in Arizona. During the Great Depression, the Chavez family lost everything. When Chavez was 10 years old, the family moved to California and became **migrant** workers. They moved from farm to farm and lived in shacks. Chavez saw the hard work his family and friends did in the fields. They were paid barely enough to live. The jobs were not safe, as the fields were often sprayed with poisons. But, his family worked 12- to 14-hour days in those fields. As a young man, Chavez saw his father and uncle join a labor union. They fought for better working conditions and pay. Chavez learned a lot from this.

Chavez spent two years in the United States Navy. Then, he went home to his family. Things had not improved, so he decided to help farm workers and their families.

Chavez worked for several labor unions. Then, he decided to start his own, called the United Farm Workers union (UFW). Its members practice nonviolence. They organize hunger strikes, church services, and marches to reach their goals.

Cesar Chavez did much to improve the lives of farm workers. He helped them get higher pay. He also helped them get better, healthier working conditions. Even after his death in 1993, his work goes on.

1. Choose another good title for this passage.

   A. Holidays

   B. Farming

   C. Join the Navy

   D. A Peaceful Leader

2. Number the following events in the order that they happened.

   _____ Chavez joins the United States Navy.

   _____ Chavez is born on a farm in Arizona.

   _____ Chavez starts the United Farm Workers union.

   _____ Chavez and his family move to California.

   _____ Chavez gets migrant workers higher pay.

3. Which of the following best defines the word **migrant**?

   A. moving

   B. happy

   C. hungry

   D. careful

4. Why do you think Chavez was such an important person?

   A. He spent two years in the United States Navy.

   B. He worked very hard.

   C. He improved the lives of farm workers.

   D. He saw his father and uncle join a labor union.

A Greek Myth

Read the myth. Then, answer the questions.

The Story of Arachne

Arachne lived in the days when all cloth was made by hand. She was famous for her spinning and weaving skills. No one wove cloth as fast or made it as **supple** and flowing.

Arachne often admired her slender hands, her long fingers, and the light, airy gauze she wove. She was certain no one could create anything as lovely. She wove **tapestries** with scenes fit for palaces.

Whenever she began to weave, people came to watch. It was like a ballet, with the threads leaping and the shuttle dancing across the loom. One day, Arachne exclaimed, "Not even the goddess Athena could teach someone to be an artist like me." Just then, an old woman in the crowd came forward. As her worn, brown robes fell away, the glittering gown of the goddess Athena appeared. But, instead of begging forgiveness, Arachne challenged Athena to a weaving contest. When they finished weaving, the onlookers could see that Arachne's work was better than the goddess's.

Athena was furious. She ripped apart Arachne's cloth and struck her with a spell. "You will weave forever, yet no one will want your tapestries on their walls." At once, Arachne's slender body became round and **bulbous**. Her long fingers turned into eight legs sprouting from her shoulders.

Arachne the spider hid until night. Only then did she dare to spin her web in a corner of the room. Alas, whenever someone found her work, they would exclaim, "Oh, another cobweb!" and brush it away.

1. Which of the following best defines the word **supple**?

    A. stiff
    B. flexible
    C. simple
    D. lovely

2. Which of the following best defines the word **bulbous**?

    A. shaped like a bulb
    B. very bumpy
    C. long
    D. thick and uneven

3. Which of the following best defines the word **tapestries**?

    A. expensive pieces of clothing
    B. woven tapes used for repairs
    C. stories told to royalty
    D. woven cloths with pictures

4. Underline the simile in paragraph three.

5. What two things are being compared in paragraph three?

    _____

6. What do you think this myth attempts to explain?

    _____

    _____

    _____

Cooking with Bread

Read each recipe. Then, complete the Venn diagram.

Grilled Cheese Sandwich
Ingredients:
- 2 slices of bread
- butter or margarine
- 1 or 2 slices of cheese
- 1 slice of ham (optional)

Directions: Butter one side of each slice of bread. Stack buttered sides together on a plate. Place cheese (and ham) onto top slice. Place skillet on burner at medium heat. Place top slice of bread with cheese (and ham) in skillet, butter side down. Place the other slice on top, butter side up. Toast until golden brown and cheese starts to melt. Flip and toast other side. When toasted evenly, remove from heat. Cut in half and serve.

French Toast
Ingredients:
- 1 egg
- $\frac{1}{4}$ tsp. (1.2 mL) vanilla
- butter or margarine
- syrup
- $\frac{1}{4}$ cup of milk
- cinnamon
- 2 slices of bread

Directions: Crack egg into bowl and beat with milk. Add $\frac{1}{4}$ tsp. (1.2 mL) vanilla and a dash of cinnamon. Place skillet on burner at medium heat. Melt margarine or butter in skillet. Dip each slice of bread into egg mixture. Place in skillet. Toast until golden brown. Flip and toast other side. When toasted evenly, remove from heat. Top with syrup and serve.

Grilled Cheese Sandwich

Both

French Toast

- uses cheese

- uses bread

- uses an egg

Fabulous Fables

Read each fable. Then, answer the questions.

A **fable** is a short story that has a moral, or lesson. This lesson can often be summarized in a single sentence. An example of a fable's moral is, "Look before you leap." That means you should always consider the consequences of an action.

The Bundle of Sticks

A man summoned his sons to give them some advice. He asked his servants to bring a bundle of sticks. He said to his oldest son, "Break it." The son strained and strained, but he was unable to break the bundle. The other sons also tried, but none of them was successful. "Untie the sticks," said the father, "and each of you take one." When they had done so, he said to them, "Now, break the sticks," and each stick was easily broken. "You see my meaning," said the father.

1. What is the moral of this fable?

   _____

   _____

   _____

2. How did the man use sticks to give his sons advice?

   _____

   _____

   _____

The Crow and the Pitcher

A thirsty crow came upon a pitcher that had once been full of water. When the crow put her beak into the mouth of the pitcher, she found that there was now very little water. She could not reach her beak far enough into the pitcher to take a drink. She almost gave up. Then, a thought came to her. She took a pebble and dropped it into the pitcher. The level of the water rose a very little bit. She took another pebble and dropped it into the pitcher. The water rose a little more. She continued to drop pebble after pebble into the pitcher. With each pebble, the water continued to rise. At last, she saw the water near the top of the pitcher. After casting in a few more pebbles, she was able to quench her thirst.

3. What is the moral of this fable?

   _____

   _____

4. How did the crow get to the water in the pitcher?

   _____

   _____

   _____

   _____

   _____

   _____

   _____

Theme Park

Read the story. Then, answer the questions.

"Let's see. Twenty-five, 50, 75, 80, 81, 82. That's $47.82,"
counted Ahmad. He gathered the change and placed it next to
the bills on the red comforter. Then, he flopped onto the bed,
making the change bounce.

"Rats! We still need $12.18 to cover the admission cost,"
pouted Zoe. "Mom said we have to have the total cost of
admission before we can go to the theme park." The brother and
sister sat on the twin beds in Ahmad's room, imagining the theme
park: games with colorful prizes, food stands with warm, salty
pretzels and crisp caramel apples, and the rides—oh, the rides!
They could almost hear the wild roller coasters, spinning swings,
and of course the Ferris wheel.

"We won't have enough for two more weeks with our
allowances," said Ahmad. "Besides, that doesn't leave any money
for food or souvenirs."

"I know," Zoe said, "and I've already checked between the
couch cushions, under the car seats, and in all of our jacket
pockets." They sat in mutual gloom and watched colorful leaves
drop outside the window to form a carpet on the lawn. Suddenly,
they had an idea.

1. What is the setting?

_____

_____

2. Who are the characters?

_____

3. What is the problem?

_____

_____

_____

4. What idea might they have at the end of the story?

_____

_____

_____

The Rosetta Stone

Read the passage. Then, answer the questions.

The Rosetta Stone was found in Egypt more than 200 years ago. It solved the mystery that puzzled historians since the time of the ancient Greeks and Romans: what do the symbols that cover the ruins of ancient Egypt mean?

The Rosetta Stone was carved and displayed around 196 B.C. It was named after the place where it was found, the town of Rosetta. Now that it has been translated, we know that it tells about King Ptolemy V of Egypt. He was king for 25 years and passed laws giving more money to the priests. In return, the priests built statues of him in all of the temples. They worshipped the statues three times a day.

Three kinds of writing that say the same thing can be found on the stone. The writing on the top part of the stone is rows of small pictures called *hieroglyphics*. Hieroglyphics were often carved on walls or on slabs of stone. Egyptian priests used hieroglyphics. The second kind of writing on the Rosetta Stone is known as **demotic**, or popular, script. It was used by the Greeks in their everyday writing—for example, to send messages. The third section, at the bottom of the stone, is written in ancient Greek.

By 196 B.C., a Greek family had ruled Egypt for more than 100 years. Because of this, the Greek alphabet and language were used in Egypt along with Egyptian writing. Modern scholars knew how to read ancient Greek. They used the stone to translate the hieroglyphic and demotic languages into ancient Greek and then into modern languages.

1. Write the main idea of the first paragraph.

_____

_____

_____

2. Write the main idea of the second paragraph.

_____

_____

_____

3. Write the main idea of the third paragraph.

_____

_____

_____

4. Write the main idea of the entire passage.

_____

_____

_____

5. Which of the following best defines the word **demotic**?

    A. angry
    B. popular
    C. written in stone
    D. language

An Unsinkable Survivor

Read the passage. Then, answer the questions.

History remembers her as the "Unsinkable Molly Brown." She survived the sinking of the cruise ship *Titanic*. Only 705 of the more than 2,200 people onboard lived through the disaster. The facts of Brown's life have almost become legendary, as some of these facts have been **exaggerated**.

Her real name was Margaret "Maggie" Tobin. Hollywood nicknamed her "Molly" after she died. Maggie grew up in Missouri near the Mississippi River. Her family was poor, and they lived in a one-bedroom house. Maggie wanted adventure and wealth. She moved to Colorado with her brother to "strike it rich" with gold.

Maggie met and married J. J. Brown in Colorado. He was an engineer who mined for gold. When he found gold, the Browns became wealthy. They began to travel, and eventually, Maggie booked passage on the *Titanic*.

On the night of April 14, 1912, the supposedly "unsinkable" *Titanic* hit a large iceberg and sank into the freezing waters of the Atlantic Ocean. The crewman in charge of Maggie's lifeboat lost hope that they would survive. But, Maggie would not let anyone give up. She made the others row to keep warm and kept their spirits high until the rescue ship arrived. Then, she helped organize rescues and made lists of survivors. She also collected donations for the survivors who did not have much money.

She got her famous nickname by saying, "Typical Brown luck. We're unsinkable."

1. What is the main idea of the second paragraph?

   A. Maggie grew up in Missouri.
   B. Maggie was poor as a child, then moved to Colorado to get rich and have some adventures.
   C. Maggie's family lived in a small house when she was young.
   D. Maggie's nickname was not really "Molly."

2. Number the following events in the order that they happened.

   _____ Maggie sailed on the *Titanic*.

   _____ Maggie married J. J. Brown.

   _____ Maggie helped with the rescues.

   _____ Maggie moved to Colorado to get rich.

   _____ Maggie grew up in Missouri near the Mississippi River.

3. Which of the following best defines the word **exaggerated**?

   A. poor
   B. stretched
   C. small
   D. dark

4. Why do you think Maggie was such a strong person?

   A. She had to be strong to overcome her poor childhood.
   B. She lifted weights as a child.
   C. A tragedy like the *Titanic* sinking makes everyone strong.
   D. She had an imagination.

Fireflies

Read the passage. Then, answer the questions.

Fireflies are **bioluminescent** insects. This means that they can produce their own light. They do this by mixing three chemicals in their bodies. One chemical is common to all living things; it is called *ATP*. The other two chemicals are called *luciferin* and *luciferase*. When these three chemicals are mixed with oxygen, the firefly is able to light its *lantern*, or the rear part of its body.

The purpose of this light is to help the firefly find a mate. Each species of firefly has a special code. The code is made of a number and length of flashes, the time between flashes, and the firefly's flight pattern while flashing. Fireflies use these unique codes to identify other members of their species.

When firefly eggs hatch, larvae emerge. The larvae are also bioluminescent and are sometimes called *glowworms*. Larvae eat during the spring, summer, and autumn months; sleep through the winter; and then progress into the next stage of their lives. They crawl into the soil where they *metamorphose*, or change, into pupae. After about two months, they emerge as adult fireflies.

Firefly light is not hot. It is, however, very bright. Catching several fireflies and putting them in a jar with air holes produces enough light to read in the dark. In some countries, fireflies are caught in nets and used as lanterns.

1. What is the topic of this passage?

   _____

   _____

2. What does the word **bioluminescent** mean?

   A. producing a sound
   B. able to produce light
   C. able to fly
   D. having chemicals in the body

3. How do fireflies produce light?

   _____

   _____

   _____

4. What is the purpose of this light?

   _____

   _____

   _____

5. Which of the following is not a stage in the firefly life cycle?

   A. egg
   B. larva
   C. tadpole
   D. pupa

The Crocodile

Read the passage and the poem. Then, use the poem to answer the questions.

Lewis Carroll is the pen name for author Charles Lutwidge Dodgson, born in England in 1832. In college, Dodgson studied both mathematics and writing. He had a very playful, witty personality. He wrote the book *Alice's Adventures in Wonderland* in 1865 and *Through the Looking-Glass* in 1872. He also wrote many poems. Dodgson wrote mostly children's literature. His writing reflects his funny, clever personality.

The Crocodile
by Lewis Carroll

How **doth** the little crocodile
Improve his shining tail,
And pour the waters of the Nile
On every golden scale!

How cheerfully he seems to grin,
How neatly spreads his claws,
And welcomes little fishes in
With gently smiling jaws!

1. What does the word **doth** mean in the first line?

    A. does

    B. does not

    C. will do

    D. had done

2. Write *T* if a statement is true. Write *F* if a statement is false.

    _____ The crocodile is taking a nap on land.

    _____ The crocodile is trying to eat the fish.

    _____ The crocodile is smiling so that the fish will swim into his mouth.

    _____ The poem is about a hungry fish.

3. Where does the poem take place?

    A. in the forest

    B. on a beach along the Pacific Ocean

    C. on a rock

    D. in the waters of the Nile

4. Why do you think the crocodile is grinning?

    _____

    _____

    _____

Marie Curie

Read the passage. Then, answer the questions.

Maria Sklodowska, a famous scientist, was born on November 7, 1867, in Warsaw, Poland. She grew up in an area of Poland where not everyone could have an education. She had an amazing memory and learned to read at the age of four.

Maria's family did not have much money but filled their home with science equipment. Her father was a professor. In 1891, Maria went to Paris to become a student at the Sorbonne. It was there, when she signed her name with the French spelling, that she became "Marie."

Marie earned her physics degree in 1893, graduating first in her class. She earned her mathematics degree in 1894, graduating second in her class. Marie met the French scientist Pierre Curie, whom she later married, in 1895. The husband and wife team became famous for their scientific work. They studied uranium's rays, which are similar to X-rays. Marie named the rays *radioactivity*. The Curies discovered two elements. When they presented their findings in 1903, Marie earned her doctorate degree. Marie Curie is the only person ever to receive the Nobel Prize in both chemistry and physics. She later became the first female professor at the Sorbonne. And, with the help of the French government and some friends and **colleagues**, she founded a radium institute. She became ill and died on July 4, 1934. Her illness was caused by her long exposure to radioactive materials.

1. How did Maria Sklodowska's name change to Marie Curie?

    A. She moved to France and decided that her name was too different.

    B. She used the French spelling of her first name and later married Pierre Curie.

    C. She changed her name so that she could leave Poland.

    D. Her best friend in Poland gave her the nickname.

2. Which statement best describes Marie Curie?

    A. She thought learning was important and useful.

    B. She did not apply herself when she was in school.

    C. She took learning for granted.

    D. She was greedy and selfish.

3. Marie Curie is the only person to

    A. become ill from radioactive materials.

    B. receive Nobel Prizes in both physics and chemistry.

    C. graduate at the top of her class in so many areas.

    D. discover an element.

4. What is Marie Curie best known for?

    _____

    _____

5. In your own words, write a definition for **colleagues**. Then, compare your definition to a dictionary's.

    _____

    _____

Early American Indians

Read the passage. Then, write the correct boldfaced word for each definition.

Some rocky land in North America is not good for farming. Without fish and game, early American Indians in those lands might have starved. Their lives were **contingent** on the animals they hunted.

These early **native** people played games. Their games **incorporated** skills they needed to survive in their **culture**. They needed to be able to judge distances. They learned to pick up clues and signs from their environment. They had to **conceal** themselves from the animals they hunted. In one of the games American Indians played, they took turns throwing spears or sticks into a hoop on the ground. Such games improved players' **accuracy**.

Moose and caribou were very important to the American Indians. Moose usually live and travel by themselves. Caribou travel in herds, covering a large area each season. American Indians **stalked** moose from one **range** to another. But, when hunting caribou, they waited at places along the caribou trails.

American Indians fished from the shore or in canoes during summer. They fished through holes cut in the ice during winter. They used **weirs**, nets, traps, hooks, and spears to catch fish. Sometimes, when meat was scarce, American Indians would eat rabbit, mink, or wolverine. When hunting became poor, they lived on dried meat, fish, and pemmican (a mixture of dried berries, dried meat, and animal fat).

1. open area upon which animals roam _____

2. combined into one _____

3. original inhabitant _____

4. dependent _____

5. pursued prey_____

6. quality of being exact _____

7. to hide _____

8. enclosures set in a waterway for catching fish _____

9. way of life _____

Louis Pasteur

Read the passage. Then, answer the questions.

Louis Pasteur, a famous scientist, was born in 1822 in France. He lived when people did not know about microscopic organisms. No one knew that there were things too small to see with the naked eye. They did not know that these tiny organisms could make people sick. People did not know that germs even existed!

Pasteur was a doctor of science but not of medicine. Because he was not a medical doctor, many medical doctors did not take his work seriously. Pasteur, however, believed strongly that germs existed and that they caused diseases.

Pasteur discovered a way to stop a disease in silkworms. He also made vaccines for the diseases rabies and anthrax. One process that he developed was named after him. It is still used today: pasteurization. This process keeps milk free from germs. Milk is heated to 140°F (60°C) for 30 minutes. The milk is then cooled quickly and sealed in sterile containers. Each time you drink a glass of cold, refreshing, germ-free milk, you have Louis Pasteur to thank.

The medical community finally recognized Pasteur's work. They invited him to speak at important medical meetings. In 1888, the Pasteur Institute opened in Paris. It is a research center. Louis Pasteur directed the work that was done there until his death in 1895. Today, more than 100 years later, scientists at the institute still build on Pasteur's ideas.

1. What did Pasteur believe that medical doctors of his time did not?

    A. He believed you could be a medical doctor without going to school.
    B. He thought the medical doctors were doing a poor job.
    C. He believed diseases were caused by germs.
    D. He wanted everyone to drink a lot of milk.

2. Which statement best describes Louis Pasteur?

    A. He was a doctor of science.
    B. He was a scientist who did not like medical doctors.
    C. He was a scientist who believed in his theories and would not quit.
    D. He was employed by dairy farmers to make milk better.

3. What is Pasteur best known for?

    A. finding that diseases are caused by germs
    B. drinking milk and having strong and healthy bones
    C. speaking at medical meetings
    D. finding a way to stop the spread of a silkworm disease

4. Write *T* if a statement is true. Write *F* if a statement is false.

    _____ Pasteur developed the process of pasteurization.

    _____ Pasteur developed a vaccine for rabies.

    _____ Pasteur developed a cure for all diseases.

    _____ Pasteur made important contributions to the progress of medicine.

Vasco da Gama

Read the passage. Then, answer the questions.

Precious stones, spices, and pearls were the treasures of India. Europeans wanted to find a way to this country by sea. But, sailing around Africa would be a long and dangerous trip.

In 1497, King Manuel I of Portugal chose Vasco da Gama to sail to India. No one wanted to sail with da Gama. Another explorer had already sailed to the southern tip of Africa, called the Cape of Good Hope, but he was not able to go any farther. His failure to reach India made others not want to try again. So, da Gama had to use men who were in jail to help sail his four ships.

Da Gama left on July 8, 1497. Four months later, he sailed past the Cape of Good Hope. The trip along the eastern coast of Africa was dangerous. The strong winds could smash the ships into the coast. Luckily, da Gama met an Indian trader who led the ships to India safely.

The trip to India was more than 11,000 miles (17,703 km) long. Often, the men were at sea for three months without setting foot on land. Some of them became sick with scurvy, an illness that comes from not eating fruits or vegetables that contain vitamin C.

Da Gama and his crew reached India on May 20, 1498. The Indian leader was friendly to them at first. But, he became angry at the quality of the gifts that da Gama brought. Da Gama was eventually forced to return to Portugal.

The return trip was worse. Many of the men did not survive because of scurvy, but da Gama made it home. He was a hero to his people.

1. Choose another good title for this passage.

   A. The Effects of Scurvy
   B. The Cape of Good Hope
   C. The Gifts for India
   D. To India by Sea

2. Why did no one want to sail with da Gama?

   _____

   _____

3. Why was the Indian leader angry with da Gama?

   _____

   _____

4. Number the following events in the order that they happened.

   _____ Da Gama and his crew reached India.

   _____ Many of da Gama's crew suffered from scurvy on the trip back to Portugal.

   _____ Da Gama was chosen to sail to India.

   _____ Da Gama sailed around the Cape of Good Hope.

5. Why do you think da Gama's men got sick with scurvy?

   A. The men did not like vegetables or fruits.
   B. The men were at sea for so long that they could not get fruits and vegetables.
   C. Most of the men had been in jail.
   D. Da Gama did not care about the crew's health.

The Play Is the Thing

Read the program. Then, answer the questions.

Belle of the Ball: A Comedy in Two Acts
by Elizabeth Weaver

Cast (in order of appearance)

Elizabeth Brown . . . . Lucy Scott

Belle Brown . . . . Meg Mitchell

Dressmaker. . . . . Susan Moore

Mr. Brown . . . . Grant Jordan

Mrs. Brown . . . . Jennifer Mills

Ernest Enderby. . . . . Michael Thompson

Clover, the family cat . . . . Clover

Guests . . . . Ry Abbot, Joe Li, Susan Moore, Ann Young

Act I

Setting: 1920s, the Brown family home, mid-afternoon.
Elizabeth and Belle Brown get ready in their **boudoir** for their
family's annual ball. The dressmaker tries to fulfill Elizabeth's rude
demands. Belle quietly puts the finishing touches on her own
dress. Mr. and Mrs. Brown talk with Ernest Enderby in the sitting
room. The girls enter the room. Clover, the family cat, comes from
under the sofa and frightens Ernest Enderby.

Act II

Setting: the ballroom, evening. Elizabeth and Belle mingle with
the guests. Belle leads the dancing until the ball is interrupted. The
guests gather on the front lawn. Ernest Enderby makes a surprising
announcement.

1. Based on the information in the program, do you think that you would enjoy this play? Why or why not?

_____

_____

_____

2. Which actor plays more than one role?
   A. Grant Jordan
   B. Lucy Scott
   C. Susan Moore
   D. Michael Thompson

3. Why might it be hard for an actor to play multiple roles?

_____

_____

_____

4. What does **boudoir** mean in the program?
   A. a small shop located at the edge of town
   B. a cellar used for storage space
   C. party decorations
   D. a woman's dressing room

5. What is the setting for Act II?

_____

_____

Duck-Billed Platypus

Read the passage. Then, answer the questions.

In the late 1700s, scientists in England received reports from Australia about the duck-billed platypus. The scientists thought that they were being tricked. They thought that a **prankster** invented this creature to fool them.

The duck-billed platypus is a unique animal. It has a bill resembling a duck's and a flat, paddle-shaped tail like a beaver. It scuffles along the ground like an alligator. Its front and hind feet are webbed and have claws. It does not have lips or exterior ears. Although it nurses its young, it does not give birth to babies. Instead, it lays eggs like a chicken. The female platypus lays two or three eggs at a time. No wonder scientists were confused! They did not know if this animal was a fish, a reptile, or a new class. They eventually classified the platypus as a mammal.

The platypus uses its bill to nuzzle in mud, searching for worms, grubs, and shellfish. It is protected while in the water by its thick, gray-brown fur. The platypus measures up to 2 feet (0.61m) in length including its tail, which is 4–5 inches (10.2–12.7 cm) long. The male is slightly larger than the female. Males have poisonous spurs on the ankle of each leg. Like a viper, the male uses these spurs to inject poison into an attacker.

The platypus is found in Australia and Tasmania. It was once hunted almost to extinction for its fur. Today, it is under the protection of the Australian government.

1. What does the duck-billed platypus use its bill for?

   A. swimming
   B. quacking
   C. searching in the mud for food
   D. defending its nest

2. What does the word **prankster** mean?

   A. someone who plays practical jokes
   B. a funny story
   C. a type of clown
   D. a funny expression

3. Write *T* if a statement is true. Write *F* if a statement is false.

   _____ The duck-billed platypus walks like an alligator.

   _____ Although the duck-billed platypus is a mammal, it lays eggs like a chicken.

   _____ The female duck-billed platypus has poisonous spurs on the ankle of each leg.

   _____ The duck-billed platypus has a tail like a beaver.

4. Circle four details in the passage that you did not know about the duck-billed platypus.

The Northern Lights

Read the story. Then, answer the questions.

It was dark. The sky was blue-black with stars winking in the distance. The nearly leafless trees stretched their shivering arms toward the sky. Meg and Maddie huddled against their mom's legs, pulling the blanket tight against the cold. They were filled with anticipation. The conditions were right; the newscaster had announced the solar winds traveling toward the earth. It just had to happen.

Orion's Belt rose slowly in the southeastern sky. The Big Dipper hovered, waiting for a scoop of color. A slight shimmer started in the west, a hint of faded blue teasing the eyes. Was it real? Slowly, the color intensified. Greens flowed through the sky like fingers from the north, reaching south and rolling in waves from east to west and back again. Then, the fingers turned red, that awesome color contrasting vividly with the velvet black sky and the waves of blue and green lights. The aurora borealis, or northern lights, shimmered spectacularly across the sky. After 10 minutes, they dimmed, faded, and disappeared. The girls sat speechless, hoping for an **encore**, but slowly the cold seeped into their awe. Shivering, they gathered their blankets and their mom's chair and walked silently into the welcoming house.

1. What time of year is it?

    _____

2. Meg, Maddie, and their mom saw the northern lights. Was it intentional or a coincidence?

    _____

3. What caused the aurora borealis?

    _____

    _____

4. Why did the girls go into the house?

    _____

    _____

5. Explain what the following phrase means: "Slowly the cold seeped into their awe."

    _____

    _____

    _____

6. What does the word **encore** mean?
    A. another one
    B. the core part
    C. the end
    D. a loud noise

Amazing Machines

Read the passage. Then, answer the questions.

Is every machine on the cutting edge? When an invention changes the way people live or complete a task, it is a breakthrough. But, many amazing machines of the past did not stay on the cutting edge. New technologies made them outdated.

The abacus was an important math invention. It is a wooden frame with beads threaded on rods. The user slides the beads to represent different numbers. Before it was invented, people counted on their fingers and kept track of numbers and totals in their heads. People used the abacus to make everyday calculations.

Another breakthrough was the printing press. Before 1450, books were rare. All books were written by hand. It usually took years to make just one book. Then, a man named Johannes Gutenberg discovered how to make *type*, or blocks with letters carved on them. He fitted the carved letters into a frame and applied ink to them. The machine pressed the inked type against paper. In 1452, Gutenberg printed 200 books. People were amazed at how quickly this invention could make books. Because of the printing press, many more people could have books and learn to read.

Computers are amazing machines. Many people can remember a time before computers existed. Now, computers are part of our everyday lives. They help run cars and fly planes. They keep track of records. Someday, people will look back and think that today's computers seem old-fashioned. Like the abacus and the printing press, one day computers will no longer seem amazing.

1. What kind of type is talked about in the passage?

    A. movements on a keyboard to make letters

    B. blocks that have letters carved on them

    C. different groups of people or animals

    D. none of the above

2. What is another way to say "on the cutting edge"?

    A. the newest technology

    B. on the edge of the knife

    C. the edge of the past

    D. using a sharp knife to cut something

3. Which of the following sentences is the best summary of the passage?

    A. Many things seem to be on the cutting edge when they are invented, but they are not.

    B. Many things are breakthroughs when they are invented, but they become part of everyday life.

    C. Amazing machines were invented long ago but not now.

    D. The abacus was a big breakthrough in math.

4. What changed because of the printing press?

    A. Before the printing press, making a book took a long time.

    B. Because of the printing press, many more people could have books and learn to read.

    C. Before type was invented, books were written by hand.

    D. all of the above

More Fabulous Fables

Read each fable. Then, answer the questions.

The Dog and the Bone

A dog found a tasty bone and was carrying it home in his mouth. On his way home, he used a wooden bridge to cross a swiftly running stream. As he crossed, he looked down and saw his reflection in the water. Thinking it was another dog with another bone, he made up his mind to have both bones. He snapped at his reflection, but as he opened his mouth, the bone fell out. It dropped into the water and was never seen again.

1. Which word best describes the dog's character?

   A. content
   B. friendly
   C. curious
   D. greedy

2. Why did the dog's bone fall into the water?

   _____

   _____

   _____

3. What is the moral of this fable?

   _____

   _____

   _____

The North Wind and the Sun

The North Wind and the Sun argued about who was more powerful. They agreed that the first one to make a traveler remove his **cloak** was the most powerful. The North Wind tried his power first and blew with all of his might. But, the harder his winds blew, the closer the traveler wrapped his cloak around himself. After using his strength, the North Wind gave up and called the Sun to try. The Sun shone with all of her warmth. As soon as the traveler felt the Sun's gentle rays, he took off his cloak.

4. What is a **cloak**?

    A. a piece of clothing similar to a coat
    B. a hat
    C. a type of glove
    D. a type of shoe

5. Why is the Sun more powerful than the North Wind?

    _____

    _____

    _____

6. What is the moral of this fable?

    A. Persuasion is better than force.
    B. Sunshine is better than wind.
    C. Always wear a coat.
    D. Swimming is fun.

Jacques Cousteau

Read the passage. Then, answer the questions.

Explorers have always traveled to new lands. By the early 1900s, explorers had walked on most of Earth's surfaces. But, Jacques Cousteau was different. He explored the world beneath the waves.

In 1936, Cousteau was in a bad car accident. He found that swimming helped him heal faster. One day, a friend lent him a pair of underwater goggles. When Cousteau put them on, he was amazed. He could see a strange, new world under the water. It was then that he decided to explore Earth's oceans.

First, Cousteau needed a way to breathe underwater for a long time. He helped invent a **device** called the Aqua-Lung. It was a tank of oxygen that a diver could wear on her back. The tank made it easy for divers to swim and stay underwater for several hours.

Cousteau began to film movies underwater. Other people could see the new world he was discovering. They could watch him explore sunken ships or find new plant and animal life.

In 1950, a millionaire gave Cousteau money to buy a ship named *Calypso*. Cousteau used this ship to do research around the world. It had special tools and an underwater room with windows.

Cousteau later had a TV series where he swam with sea animals, including sharks, eels, and octopuses. People saw that these animals were not monsters and that they were usually afraid of humans.

Cousteau not only taught people about the oceans, but he also worked hard to protect the environment. He wanted future generations to enjoy the many wonders he found beneath the water.

1. Choose another good title for this passage.

   A. Sharks, Eels, and Octopuses
   B. Exploring beneath the Waves
   C. Movies under the Sea
   D. Protecting the Environment

2. What was the name of Cousteau's ship?

   _____

3. What did Cousteau use to teach the world about sea creatures?

   _____

   _____

4. Which of the following best defines the word **device**?

   A. a clamp
   B. a hose
   C. a snorkel
   D. a tool

5. Why do you think that Cousteau wanted other people to see the new world that he was discovering?

   A. so that they would buy the Aqua-Lung he invented
   B. so that they would watch his television series
   C. so that they would help protect the oceans
   D. so that they would stay away from sharks

Sacagawea

Read the passage. Then, answer the questions.

The United States has gold dollar coins. On one type of those coins is the image of a young American Indian woman and her baby. The young woman's name is Sacagawea.

In 1800, an enemy tribe captured Sacagawea. She was only about 11 years old. The tribe took her far away from her Shoshone home and made her a slave. Then, she was married to a fur trader.

Four years later, Sacagawea joined a group of explorers led by Meriwether Lewis and William Clark. They wanted to find a way to the Pacific Ocean across northwestern America. They hired Sacagawea and her husband because she knew the land and people they would cross along the way. Sacagawea went with her baby son strapped to her back.

Without Sacagawea's help, the trip may not have been a success. One day, the explorers' journals fell out of a canoe into a river. Sacagawea jumped into the water to get them. If she had not saved them, we might not know as much about Lewis and Clark's explorations. She was their interpreter when they met different American Indian tribes. In August 1805, the explorers met a group of Shoshones. Sacagawea quickly saw that the chief was her brother. Her people welcomed her back. They gave the explorers food, supplies, and horses to continue their journey.

The explorers returned home safely. They succeeded as a result of Sacagawea's help. Now, this brave American Indian woman is on a gold dollar coin.

1. What is the main idea of the fourth paragraph?

   A. Sacagawea helped the explorers have a successful trip.
   B. The explorers made discoveries during the journey.
   C. The life of a Shoshone woman was hard.
   D. Sacagawea saw the Pacific Ocean.

2. About how old was Sacagawea when an enemy tribe captured her?

   _____

3. What area did Lewis and Clark hope to explore?

   _____

4. What is the value of the coin that has Sacagawea's image?

   _____

5. Into what American Indian tribe was Sacagawea born?

   _____

6. Number the following events in the order that they happened.

   _____ Sacagawea found her brother.

   _____ Sacagawea was kidnapped.

   _____ Sacagawea joined the Lewis and Clark expedition.

   _____ Sacagawea saved the explorers' journals when they fell into a river.

   _____ Sacagawea was married.

The Brain

Read the passage. Then, answer the questions.

The human brain is complicated. Your brain controls everything about you. It keeps your heart beating. It tells your body how to move. It keeps your body at the right temperature. It helps you see, feel, taste, hear, and smell. Your brain stores your memories. It is the place where all of your thoughts and ideas begin.

The brain is not very big. This is surprising since it does so much. But, this critical organ, or body part, only weighs about three pounds (1.4 kg). It makes up less than two percent of your whole body. Yet, without it, nothing in your body would work.

How does the brain do all of its work? It sends messages to every part of the body by using **neurons**, or nerve cells. Neurons use a linking method, called *synapses*, to send information from the brain to other parts of the body. Synapses are the tiny spaces between the neurons. More than 100 billion neurons are in your brain. They send commands across 1 quadrillion synapses.

Even when you are asleep, your brain works. It makes you dream. It tells your heart to keep beating and your lungs to keep breathing. It wakes you if you hear a loud noise, if you feel something strange, or if you have had enough sleep.

Different parts of the brain manage different parts of the body. The upper part of your brain, shaped like a bike helmet, takes care of memories and feelings. The lower part of your brain controls your body movements. The brain stem, in the lower back of the brain, is in charge of things like your heart, blood movement, and hunger.

1. What are synapses like?

   A. safety ropes B. nerves
   C. tiny gaps between wires D. big holes in the road

2. Why is it surprising that the brain only weighs three pounds (1.4 kg)?

   A. It is surprising because that is very heavy.
   B. It is surprising because the brain does so much work but is so small.
   C. It is surprising that the brain does not weigh less.
   D. It is surprising that the brain needs so much room.

3. What are **neurons**?

   A. connections between cells B. nerve cells
   C. linking systems D. memory cells

4. What does your brain control?

   A. the beating of your heart
   B. your body temperature
   C. the movement of your body
   D. all of the above

5. Write *T* if a statement is true. Write *F* if a statement is false.

   _____ Your dreams are created by your brain.

   _____ The brain stem controls your thoughts and feelings.

   _____ The upper part of the brain is shaped like a ball.

   _____ Neurons are linked by synapses.

   _____ The lower part of your brain controls body movements.

Ships of the Desert

Read the passage. Then, use the details listed below to complete the chart.

Camels were once wild animals in Arabia and Asia. But, they were domesticated long ago. The two kinds of camels are the one-humped Arabian camel and the two-humped Bactrian camel. Both are useful animals. But, Bactrian camels are sturdier. They can carry heavier loads and withstand cooler climates. Arabian camels have shorter hair than Bactrian camels. They can also be trained for racing.

Camels are called "ships of the desert." This is because they walk with a swaying motion like a ship sways on the water. They are also a major mode of transportation in the desert.

A camel's hump is made of fat. The camel's body uses the fat for food when plants are not available on long desert journeys. Water is not stored in a camel's hump. Water is stored in body tissues and in pouches inside a camel's stomach.

Nomadic people in North Africa and Asia still use camels. Camels carry loads where there are no roads. But, they are not only used for transportation. Their hair, hides, meat, and milk are used for clothing and food.

used for food and clothing

can withstand cooler climates

one hump

trained for racing

stores water in body tissue and stomach pouches

sturdier

two humps

shorter hair

walk with a swaying motion

hump stores fat

Arabian Camel	Bactrian Camel	Both
_____	_____	_____
_____	_____	_____
_____	_____	_____
_____	_____	_____
_____	_____	_____
_____	_____	_____
_____	_____	_____
_____	_____	_____

Cause and Effect

Read each paragraph. Then, answer the questions.

A **cause** is something that creates a result. An **effect** is what happens as a result of something.

Tien sat on the swing. Juan walked behind him. Juan grabbed the swing in both hands, pulled as he backed up, ran forward, and pushed the swing as hard as he could. Tien rode up, soared through the air, and came whooshing back down.

1. What caused Tien to go forward?

   _____

2. What was the effect of Tien's going forward?

   _____

   _____

Jan set her lunch bag on the seat of the bus. She turned to talk to a friend, bumping the bag onto the floor. Her apple rolled four seats forward. Her popcorn scattered everywhere. Jan watched as her plastic water bottle bounced three times, then burst.

3. What caused Jan's lunch bag to fall to the floor?

   _____

4. What was the effect of the bottle bouncing three times?

   _____

Ana wanted a puppy. She wrote a plan detailing how she would pay and care for the new pet. Then, she proved her responsibility by helping with household chores for a month. Her parents were so impressed, they agreed to the new addition to the family.

5. What caused Ana to write a plan?

   _____

6. What was the effect of Ana's helping with chores?

   _____

   _____

Pavel set his alarm for 7:30 A.M. so that he would have half an hour to finish his homework in the morning. He went to sleep. That night, there was a thunderstorm. The power went out for five minutes, then came back on. The next morning, Pavel's mom called him for breakfast at 8:00 A.M. Pavel could not believe it. His alarm did not go off. He had to rush to get ready for school and finish his homework.

7. What caused the power to go out?

   _____

8. What was the effect of Pavel's alarm not going off?

   _____

   _____

Figures of Speech

Circle the best meaning for each underlined idiom.

An **idiom** is a figure of speech. An idiom has a different meaning than the exact meaning of the individual words.

1. Father asked Cara to be quiet. Ian tried to bother her. Cara should ignore Ian or she would <u>play right into his hands</u>.

   A. put hands on her shoulders
   B. fall into a trap that someone plans for hidden motives
   C. make noise by playing hand instruments
   D. play a game involving the hands

2. While Maria was reading her novel, she <u>ran across</u> the date World War II began.

   A. moved quickly across a library
   B. crossed out the dates
   C. happened to find something
   D. saw something while running

3. Adrian thought he was too old to help with the scavenger hunt. Melina told him to <u>let his hair down</u> and join in the fun.

   A. untie his hair
   B. relax
   C. brush his hair
   D. try a new hairstyle

Staying On Topic

Underline the sentence that does not belong in each paragraph.

1. This article discusses household measuring tools. Thermometers are found in water heaters, ovens, and microwaves. Carpets help keep your feet warm. Measuring cups and spoons are in nearly every kitchen. Clocks can be found in bedrooms, kitchens, and living rooms.

2. I read an article about rain forest plants. Animals like monkeys and sloths live in rain forests. Numerous flowering plants and vines grow on the forest floor. Many of the trees grow as high as city buildings. Bromeliads are plants that grow in a rain forest's canopy.

3. "Today's Computers" talks about the many uses of computers. They are used to access the Internet. Computers are used to write reports, letters, and schoolwork. They are also used to play recreational and educational computer games. Computers can come in different colors.

4. This brochure lists some of the reactions people can have to anesthesia. Shaking is one reaction. Other people become sleepy for several hours after surgery. Anesthesia makes surgery easier for people because they do not remember any of the pain. Another reaction is becoming grouchy.

Predicting Outcomes

Read each paragraph. Then, answer the questions.

To predict means to use clues to guess what will happen next.

Jayla was 80 years old. She lived in a house with a very small, fenced-in yard. She decided to get a dog from the animal shelter. She narrowed her choice to two dogs. One dog was a large retriever. He had a lot of energy and was used to running on acres of land. The other dog was a small mixed breed. He was used to staying inside and knew how to use a doggy door to go outside.

1. Which dog do you think Jayla will choose?

   _____

2. Why do you think she will make that choice?

   _____

Harry's weekend was busy. He spent Friday night at Justin's house. They stayed up late. Harry left early the next morning for baseball practice. He was tired when he got home. But, he helped his mom get ready for her party that evening. When the preparations were finished, Harry decided to take a nap.

3. What do you think will happen next?

   _____

4. Explain your answer.

   _____

Drawing Conclusions

Read each paragraph. Circle the clothing item or accessory that each paragraph describes. Write the clues that helped you decide.

1. Sharon needed something to carry on her trip. She wanted it to be large enough to hold her money, glasses, address book, and small cosmetic bag. She preferred that it have a shoulder strap and go with all of the clothes she was taking.

   A. wallet   B. purse
   C. suitcase   D. backpack

   What clues made you select this accessory?

   _____

   _____

   _____

2. Albie went to buy something he could wear to cool off and relax at the beach. He found the perfect thing—it was dark blue with little yellow fish around each leg opening.

   A. beach towel   B. tennis shorts
   C. swimsuit   D. golf shirt

   What clues made you select this item?

   _____

   _____

   _____

Word Bridges

Circle the name of a food hidden in each sentence. Each hidden word bridges at least two separate words. Then, write the food name.

1. Sal added the numbers. _____

2. Bob read the book. _____

3. Visit me at the zoo. _____

4. All I'm eating is a bun. _____

5. The busy bee told a story. _____

6. Peg got an A on the test. _____

7. The whales at the cape are huge! _____

8. The stuffed, little monster is cute. _____

Choose two foods. Write two word bridge sentences using the food names as hidden words. Give your sentences to a friend to solve.

9. _____

   _____

10. _____

   _____

In Other Words

Write as many words as you can using the letters from each word below.

elephant	hippopotamus
_____	_____
_____	_____
_____	_____
_____	_____
_____	_____

computers	reading
_____	_____
_____	_____
_____	_____
_____	_____
_____	_____

Wise Words

Write the letter of each proverb next to its meaning.

A **proverb** is a wise or thoughtful saying.

A. A friend in need is a friend indeed.
B. Do not change horses in midstream.
C. Many hands make light work.
D. Half a loaf is better than none.
E. Do not cry over spilled milk.
F. The grass is always greener on the other side.
G. Make hay while the sun shines.

1. _____ Do not change your mind once you have begun to do something.

2. _____ Do not procrastinate. Get your work done when you should.

3. _____ Getting part of something is better than not getting any of it.

4. _____ No matter what you have, you always think that what someone else has is better.

5. _____ Things get done easily when everyone helps.

6. _____ When someone wants something, he acts like a good friend so that you will help him.

7. _____ When you make a mistake, do not dwell on it.

More Than One Meaning

Write the homograph for each pair of definitions in the boxes below. Then, unscramble the shaded letters to answer the trivia question.

> **Homographs** are words that are spelled the same but have different meanings. Sometimes, they also sound different.

1. not absent/a gift
2. to protest/something that can be touched
3. to close tightly/a sea animal
4. fresh fruit and vegetables/to manufacture
5. a baseball player/a mixture of eggs, flour, and milk
6. to go well together/used to start a fire
7. to crowd or squeeze/a game played in a four-walled court
8. tiny/60 seconds
9. historical account/to document
10. to abandon/dry, sandy region
11. firm and steady/where horses live

1.
2.
3.
4.
5.
6.
7.
8.
9.
10.
11.

What popular snack food was invented by George Crum?

_____ _____ _____ _____ _____ _____   _____ _____ _____ _____ _____

Answer Key

Page 5
1. A.; 2. They mixed features of humans and animals.; 3. T, F, F, T; 4. Olmec rulers; 5. their skills in architecture, pottery, art, mathematics, and astronomy

Page 7
1. C.; 2. Answers will vary.; 3. Answers will vary, but may include: dark and somber, determined, or pitiful.; 4. Answers will vary but may include: shadow, shade, and fell.; 5. C.

Pages 8–9
1. F; 2. O; 3. O; 4. F; 5. F; 6. O; 7. F; 8. O; 9. F; 10. O

Page 11
1. D.; 2. A.; 3. 5, 4, 1, 2, 3; 4. Answers will vary.; 5. New York; 6. five; 7. almost three months

Pages 12–13
1. 4; 2. Answers will vary but may include: bar graphs are easy to read and they make it easy to compare data.; 3. 3; 4. 5 minutes; 5. 125 beats per minute; 6. Answers will vary but may include: line graphs are easy to read and they make it easy to show changes in data over time.

Page 15
1. It lives in the Indian and South Pacific oceans, from 60 feet to 1,500 feet deep (also, in the outermost chamber of its shell).; 2. It is a living fossil related to the octopus and squid. It has an external, chambered shell and 80–100 tentacles around its head.; 3. tiny fish, shrimp, molted shells of lobsters; 4. Circle the following: They have tentacles. They live in the ocean. They lay eggs.; 5. Underline the following: They have external shells. They cannot change color. They do not squirt ink. They live longer.

Page 17
1. C.; 2. near where Kentucky, Tennessee, and Virginia meet; 3. hunted, fished, and carried dried staples; 4. B.; 5. Daniel Boone and about 30 woodsmen; 6. late 1700s

Page 19
1. The swirling snow blurred the landscape.; 2. D.; 3. blowing snow; 4. Nina fell backward into the snow.; 5. A.; 6. Tiny was standing on her back.

Pages 20–21
1. R; 2. F; 3. F; 4. R; 5. F; 6. R; 7. R; 8. F; 9. R; 10. R; 11.–12. Answers will vary.

Page 23
1. D.; 2. 4, 1, 2, 3, 5; 3. A.; 4. C.

Page 25
1. D.; 2. 3, 1, 4, 2, 5; 3. A.; 4. C.

Answer Key

2. A.; 3. D.; 4. It was like a
~~et~~, with the threads leaping
~~a~~d the shuttle dancing across the
~~r~~oom.; 5. a ballet and weaving;
6. Answers will vary but may
include: the origin of spiders and
spider webs.

Page 29
French Toast: uses cinnamon, milk,
an egg, vanilla, and syrup. Grilled
Cheese Sandwich: uses cheese and
ham. Both: use bread and butter or
margarine.

Pages 30–31
1. strength in numbers; 2. People
are stronger if they stay together,
just like the sticks are harder to
break when they are all together.;
3. Persistence is the key to solving
problems.; 4. The crow dropped
pebbles into the pitcher until the
water was high enough to drink.

Page 33
1. Ahmad's bedroom; 2. Ahmad and
Zoe; 3. They do not have enough
money for admission to the theme
park.; 4. Answers will vary but may
include: They will rake leaves to earn
the money.

Page 35
Answers will vary but may include:
1. The Rosetta Stone was found in
Egypt more than 200 years ago.;
2. The Rosetta Stone tells about
King Ptolemy V.; 3. There are
three different kinds of writing on
the stone.; 4. The Rosetta Stone
unlocked the mystery that puzzled
historians since the time of the
ancient Greeks and Romans: what
did the symbols say that covered
the temples and tombs of ancient
Egypt?; 5. B.

Page 37
1. B.; 2. 4, 3, 5, 2, 1; 3. B.; 4. A.

Page 39
1. fireflies; 2. B.; 3. They mix three
chemicals in their bodies.; 4. It helps
them find mates.; 5. C.

Page 41
1. A.; 2. F, T, T, F; 3. D.; 4. Answers
will vary.

Page 43
1. B.; 2. A.; 3. B.; 4. her scientific
work with radioactive substances;
5. Answers will vary.

Page 45
1. range; 2. incorporated; 3. native;
4. contingent; 5. stalked; 6. accuracy;
7. conceal; 8. weirs; 9. culture

Page 47
1. C.; 2. C.; 3. A.; 4. T, T, F, T

Page 49
1. D.; 2. They heard stories about
another explorer's failed voyage.;
3. He was unhappy with Da Gama's
gifts.; 4. 3, 4, 1, 2; 5. B.

Page 51
1. Answers will vary.; 2. C.; 3. Answers
will vary but may include: More than
one role might mean quick costume
and makeup changes, as well as bring
the challenges of changing characters
and remembering more lines.; 4. D.;
5. the ballroom, evening

Answer Key

Page 53
1. C.; 2. A.; 3. T, T, F, T; 4. Answers will vary.

Page 55
1. late autumn; 2. intentional; 3. solar winds traveling toward the earth; 4. They were cold, and the northern lights were over.; 5. The cold slowly brought them out of their amazement.; 6. A.

Page 57
1. B.; 2. A.; 3, B.; 4. D.

Pages 58–59
1. D.; 2. He opened his mouth to grab the second bone.; 3. Be happy with what you have.; 4. A.; 5. He was able to make the traveler take off his cloak.; 6. A.

Page 61
1. B.; 2. *Calypso*; 3. his television series; 4. D.; 5. C.

Page 63
1. A.; 2. about 11 years old; 3. northwest America; 4. $1.00; 5. Shoshone; 6. 5, 1, 3, 4, 2

Page 65
1. C.; 2. B.; 3. B.; 4. D.; 5. T, F, F, T, T

Page 67
Arabian Camel: one hump, trained for racing, shorter hair; Bactrian Camel: can withstand cooler climates, sturdier, two humps; Both: water stored in body tissue and stomach pouches, used for food and clothing, swaying motion, hump stores fat

Pages 68–69
1. Juan pushed his swing.; 2. came whooshing back down.; 3. bumped it.; 4. It burst.; 5. She rea wanted a puppy.; 6. Her parents decided to let her get a puppy.; 7. The thunderstorm caused the power to go out.; 8. Pavel had to rush to get ready for school and finish his homework.

Page 70
1. B.; 2. C.; 3. B.

Page 71
1. Carpets help keep your feet warm.; 2. Animals like monkeys and sloths live in rain forests.; 3. Computers can come in different colors.; 4. Anesthesia makes surgery easier for people because they do not remember any of the pain.

Page 72
Answers will vary.

Page 73
1. B.; 2. C.

Page 74
1. salad; 2. bread; 3. meat; 4. lime, meat; 5. beet; 6. egg; 7. pear; 8. lemon; 9–10. Answers will vary.

Page 75
Answers will vary.

Page 76
1. B.; 2. G.; 3. D.; 4. F.; 5. C.; 6. A.; 7. E.

Page 77
1. present; 2. object; 3. seal; 4. produce; 5. batter; 6. match; 7. squash; 8. minute; 9. record; 10. desert; 11. stable; potato chips